"Hello My Name is Wayne"

From Socializing to Check Cashing; Relationship Marketing That Works!

by

Wayne R. Weld

ISBN-13:978-1507738320

"Technology will never replace a handshake, a hug, or a kind word."
Jordan Adler

Forward

Every street and road in every city and town in America, and the world for that matter, has businesses that need to attract and keep customers. The more high tech society becomes, with the internet, the harder it is for "normal" marketing and advertising to deliver. The effectiveness of marketing and advertising dollars has diminished. " Social Media" is today's Golden Goose.

And the shift is on. People more and more use the internet (Google, Yahoo, Yelp, Craig's List, etc.) for product and service information; information that used to be provided by sales people. Now the clients and customers are already informed on the product or service they want and are much freer as to where they make their purchase.

The Old is New Again

What has been labeled "old fashioned" today is now, to

the contrary, more important and newer than ever. In our high tech age, effective personal communication is increasingly difficult, although it would seem otherwise with email, texting, voice mail, newsletters, e-blasts, web sites, blogs, etc. Most people are in high-tech overload.

Today the "delete" button is the most used key on the computer.

As always, today's business must have a firm grasp on personal contact and the fundamentals of relationship marketing in order to survive and prosper.

In the words of William James: "The deepest principle of human nature is the craving to be appreciated." This craving is best met by developing relationships one on one/face to face over time. Relationships are where business comes from, referrals come from and friendships come from. This book is about how to make that happen.

Its purpose is to provide a prospect/client - partner acquisition plan and follow up system that works in real life.

With it, an astute business person, can expect to build his/her business to the point where 80+% of their ever increasing income will be generated by relatively few referral partners... their Super Star referral partners.

This Book offers a Long Term Plan for Huge Success.

In a short period of time, you can:

- Realize "off the charts" business, earning huge repetitive income...
- Have lunch 30-50 weeks a year with business friends who are stark raving fans...
- Enjoying your extensive free time...

How?

By learning and implementing this world class contact and follow up system... relationship marketing!

The plan and focus consists of skills in two parts:

- Business Networking skills, and
- Effective Follow Up skills.

The two used in combination will provide meaningful

long lasting business and personal relationships, and in this case, business networking is the driving force.

This book is short and sweet, as the "how to" is short and sweet; meet new people, develop meaningful relationships.

You will be able to evaluate and implement the suggestions immediately.

While this book is specific in its intent; building strong business relationships... through skillful networking and skillful follow up. It <u>does not cover</u> many of the other necessary areas of knowledge for success that a prosperous entrepreneur needs to possess: i.e.:

- Positive Attitude
- Continuous Personal Development
- Financial Planning/Budgeting
- Product Development
- Systems and Processes
- Recruiting and Training
- Overall Marketing/Advertising
- Sales Training
- Customer Service

These, and other business techniques and philosophies, can all be gleaned from the suggested reading list in the Appendix. The topics are important to a thriving business and should be studied well.

But nothing yields stronger more lasting and impactful results than strong relationships... You can obtain this, in large part, from using these effective networking and proven follow up strategies.

Join Those Who Cash Checks!

Part One

<u>NET</u>WORKING

(The Fun Part)

PART ONE: <u>INITIATING SUCCESSFUL CONTACTS</u>
<u>(the **FUN** part!)</u>

Connecting/Building Relationships:
Getting Started

All activities, both formal and informal, that bring you into contact with a potential client or partner is networking. i.e. business events, standing in line in the grocery store, attending sporting events, grabbing a coffee at a local coffee shop, etc.

The objective is simple; to find a potential referral partner (with whom to form a strategic alliance) and/or to find a client or customer. You're looking for the few people who are, or will become, your Super Stars.

This book is geared towards meeting people at networking events, but applies to any situation resulting in meeting a new potential Super Star.

NETWORKING/CONNECTING PREPERATION:

1. Reconnect with old friends (business connections, classmates, family, long lost friends, neighbors, etc.). Develop a full list with email addresses, web sites, Facebook pages, Google+ circles, real mailing addresses, birthdays and other significant information. (see examples in the Appendix)

Relationship Marketing That Works!

2. Start a "Super Star Connection Fund". Create a separate business or personal budget category, funded regularly, for networking funds so that you will always be able to take someone important to lunch or out for coffee or attend an important event.

3. Make a list of your current "Super Stars" of super connectors; your Super Stars who provided you with at least one referral in the past year.

4. Expand your view as to where to find opportunities to build your list.

HINT: Go Where Your Prospects Go!

* Charity Events   * Industry Classes
* Cultural Events   * Restaurants
* Trade Shows   * Neighborhood Associations
* Private Clubs   * Business Journal Events
* Prospects' Assoc.   * Self Development Classes
* General Bus. Events * etc.

A. Have your networking strategy in hand before you attend an event.
B. Schedule 1-2 events per month to attend.

Put your prime networking events on your calendar for the year... business networking meetings, Chamber Events, etc. At the same time schedule your follow up activity. This way you will not have conflicts or double bookings.

C. List 1-2 prime people you want to meet at each event as it approaches.
D. See Networking Event Tip #7

Be ready to network when you arrive. Know and use the networking tips that follow.

Follow up plans are targeted to 3 groups

a. Good clients and referral partners that like you and are giving you referrals (Super Stars). The "A" list.

b. Strong prospects that you think will be exceptional "partners" in the future; Super Stars who may provide one or more referrals per year. The "B" list.

x. The other 80% to 90% ("x" list) which you know, but who will probably not reciprocate in a positive way. Eliminate using this "x" list.

THE SITUATION:

Consider this. You are attending a business networking event tomorrow and wish that the results would be noticeably productive. i.e. you want to finish the meeting with some real prospects that you know to be of high value, not just socialize with a couple of friends. To get better results, you need a better (professional) approach.

Tips for an Effective Network Meeting Experience

Use as many of these tips as possible which fit the event you're attending.

NETWORKING EVENT *TIP #1*: Have a plan & objective for the event i.e. leave with 3 appointments with people of Super Star potential.

> *Like anything else, you are more proactive and focused with a goal and a plan. Know why you're there and what you wish to accomplish while you are there... or stay home.*

NETWORKING EVENT *TIP #2*: Show up early, stay to the end.

If the event is worth attending, then maximize your time by, first attending the whole event. That way you will have a chance with everyone; those that come early and leave early and those that attend late and stay late.

NETWORKING EVENT TIP #3: <u>Walk the entire room at least twice.</u>

Be mobile. Be sure to cover the ground. Various people tend to congregate in specific areas of comfort, i.e. by the bar, by the food, over by the stage, by the door, etc. Make it a point to move around so that you have the chance to speak to all.

NETWORKING EVENT TIP #4: <u>Target prospects before you arrive... what top 3 prospects do you want to meet?</u>

If you are familiar with the group, or are part of it, you probably already know who the important members are. If the group contains current or future Super Stars, be sure to enhance your connections and include them in your follow up plan. If this is your 1st visit to a new group you do not know, refer to **NETWORKING EVENT TIP #24: <u>BONUS</u>**

NETWORKING EVENT TIP #5: <u>Spend 80% of your time with people you do not know... only 20% or less with those you do.</u>

> *This is not an exact number, but the primary reason for attending the event is to meet new people (looking for Super Stars), and only incidentally to 'catch up' with friends. Make it a point to talk with strangers.*

NETWORKING EVENT TIP #6: <u>At the beginning and end of the event, position yourself near the entrance where you can see everyone coming and going. This allows you to see most people at least twice.</u>

> *This is a good technique for insuring that you see everyone. If it is important enough to attend, it is important enough to give it your full attention.*

NETWORKING EVENT TIP #7: <u>Have your quick (15 seconds) "infomercial" down pat.</u> (Not what you do, but the problems you solve.)... your "Why."

> *Don't be caught in the trap of spouting a bunch of facts and figures about how great you and your company are, no one cares. You will be tuned out*

quickly. But they do care, and are curious about, what problems you solve. For example: "I'm Wayne. I assist businesses to implement world class follow-up systems that directly adds money to their bottom line."

NETWORKING EVENT TIP #8: <u>Say the other person's name at least three times during the conversation.</u>

There is not a more pleasant sound to a person than the sound of their own name. By making a point (and habit) of using their name you are much more likely to be remembered. Also you are much more likely to remember them.

NETWORKING EVENT TIP #9: <u>Be happy and enthusiastic.</u>

No one wants to hang out or talk with someone who is negative or complains. If you have issues, leave them at home. Much better to be happy and enthusiastic.

NETWORKING EVENT TIP #10: <u>Eat before you arrive or after you leave, and don't drink.</u>

Unless you are going to a dinner function, leave the food and alcohol alone. You are there for business. It is difficult to look professional while balancing a drink and hors d'oeuvres, trying to focus on the other individual and taking notes... all at the same time.

NETWORKING EVENT TIP #11: <u>Stay until the end.</u>

Maximize you opportunities. You can typically have some of your best conversations when the room starts to thin out and you have someone's undivided attention.

NETWORKING EVENT TIP #12: <u>1ˢᵗ establish rapport... try to create an instant history; find common grounds.</u> (**"F.O.R.M."** = **F**amily, **O**ccupation, **R**ecreation, **M**otivation or **M**oney.) <u>See Appendix.</u>

By just spending a few minutes asking questions and discussing family, occupations, recreation and motivation, some common ground can be established quickly. With common interests or history... or a genuine interest in areas you don't have in common, you will leave a good impression and will have created a knowledge base that will be useful later.

NETWORKING EVENT TIP #13: <u>Don't give out your</u>

information too soon.

Avoid the temptation to explain yourself... me, me, and me. The old adage is true, "no one cares how much you know until they know how much you care." There is a time and place for everything. Details about what you do don't belong at the beginning.

NETWORKING EVENT TIP #14: Write pertinent information on the back of the prospect's card immediately so you can review later.

By the end of the evening you will have spoken with many people. It is much easier to follow up effectively and personally if you have retained some of the important information gained in the encounters. If space permits, the back of their business card is a good place for that information.

NETWORKING EVENT TIP #15: Don't try to sell your service; Sell a mutual appointment within the next 7 days... a One on One.

With time limited at the event, it is usually pointless to try to get into any details that will be meaningful in a brief conversation; as you want to develop a personal relationship anyway. Instead it should be the objective of the encounter to continue the conversation later in private. The most effective approach is to schedule a coffee One on One within the next few days.

NETWORKING EVENT TIP #16: Don't waste time on people who are not good prospects.

It is important to be friendly and interested in all. However make sure that opportunities do not slip away spending too much time with people that are not optimal sources for you.

NETWORKING EVENT TIP #17: Be aware of time... 3-5 minutes per person.

It is easy to let time run out. In a 2 hour event at 5 minutes per person you will chat with 24 people... many may be your friends that want to catch up for 15-20 minutes. Make sure you have enough time available for the important people you wish to engage.

NETWORKING EVENT TIP #18: Know the kind of problems you can solve, not a bunch of boring facts about your service.

We've all been there: "Hi, I'm Joe, here's my card, I'm with ABC and we do XYZ and blah blah blah blah." We can't put them in the rear view mirror quick enough! In the course of your conversation, when it comes up, quickly highlight the problems you solve; do not try to sell your product or service. Remember, your objective is a follow up meeting.

NETWORKING EVENT TIP #19: Learn how to <u>make small talk, important talk</u>.

Remember F.O.R.M. in Tip #12. At this stage it is much more important to bond than to sell. In fact that is always the case.

NETWORKING EVENT TIP #20: At breakfasts and luncheons and dinners, <u>always try to sit with 3 people you don't know.</u>

At a meal function you will be anchored in one spot for an hour or more; a perfect opportunity to spend time with new people; the reason you are there. While it is fun and comfortable to chat with friends, it is counterproductive to your purpose.

NETWORKING EVENT TIP #21: <u>Have a follow-up plan,</u> i.e. within 24 hours invite the prospect to join you on Facebook, LinkedIn, and Twitter, Send an email expressing gratitude, and send a personal greeting card. In combination, these are very effective. (Send one card free at: <u>www.sendoutcards.com/LTD</u>), schedule a One on One coffee, Office visit etc.

> *Don't lose any advantage you may have earned by burning through people with shoddy skills and follow up. The critical piece of all this activity in making contacts is implementing a <u>world class</u> follow up plan... without follow-up, making all the good contacts in your networking activity is of little value. Would you do business with someone you just met that you never heard from again?*

(Follow Up is the subject of Part Two.)

NETWORKING EVENT TIP #22: <u>Keep in mind; it is "Network" not "Net-sit," "Net-eat" or "Net-drink."</u>

Be professional. Have a plan, follow your plan.

NETWORKING EVENT TIP #23: <u>Purchase, study, learn:</u> <u>Jeffrey Gitomer's book "The Little Black Book of</u>

Connections," Michael J. Maher's "The 7 Levels of Communication" and "Straight-Line Leadership" by Dusan Dyukich

As enumerated in suggestions for reading material in the Appendix, they are all very beneficial. I suggest starting with these three.

NETWORKING EVENT TIP #24: BONUS
Your Secret Weapon; the professional approach!

The first time attending a new group there are many different approaches. The following is easy and easily the simplest.

Every event, whether it is a business meeting or your family Thanksgiving meal, has an organizer, has a person who has a vested interest and wants everyone to have a good time (a memorable experience).

This person might be the business host, the party host, the cook at a house party, the minister at church; the Happy Hour host, or whoever... but there is always someone who wants the event to be successful. This will be true of every event.

The point is that this represents an opportunity for you.

When first arriving to the event, find the organizer/host and introduce yourself. Remember, he/she wants you to be happy and have a good experience. It goes something like this...

> *"Hello, my name is _____ . This is my first time here and I love this event. My service is _____, and I build my business by providing quality service, and by also giving referral business to those folks I think provide quality service to their clients as well. You know the people here. Who would you suggest are the top 3 connectors here tonight, who would you like to know? Would you be kind enough to introduce me to them?"*

That's it! In a matter of minutes you will be introduced to the most important people in the room, with a third party endorsement. You then simply use your skills to begin building the relationship, to find out pertinent information and to set up a follow up appointment. Note: this does not prove effective on your second visit!

Common Sense: It is a good bet that you are not attending this event looking for someone to buy something from.

Conversely, it's also a good bet no one in the room came there to buy something from you!

So leading with a conversation about your company, your product, your pricing etc. is the worst of all possible approaches.

On top of that, no one cares initially what you do; plus the sales barriers are now up. If you start selling, anything you say from that point on, just digs the hole you started, deeper! It's about relationships first; finding referral collaborators and sales later. Act accordingly.

Top questions you may want to prepare in advance to make small talk important talk...

- Where did you grow up? How did you get from there to here?
- What made you choose your career?
- What are you the most proud of?
- What's the question that you wish people would ask, but don't?
- What do you do in your free time for fun?

Networking is not about collecting 30 business cards; networking is all about finding 1-2 quality contacts... and then doing something important with those 1-2.
Let's see what those important activities might be!

HINT – Follow up is always the name of the game! Be sure you secure the necessary information at the networking event that you will need for follow up.

This ends Part One... identify a few new friends.

Join Those Who Cash Checks!

Part Two

NET**WORK**ING

(The Work Part)

PART TWO: EFFECTIVE FOLLOW UP
(the **WORK** part!)

Skill Development

If you only learn one skill in your career from this time forward, make effective follow up that skill.

It is easy to attend events, eat, drink, talk to friends and a few strangers; then kid yourself that something was actually accomplished! In fact, probably, nothing was accomplished except for wasting time and money.

Most leave an event with a hand full of business cards which are entered into an email list and the individuals are 'friended' on Facebook or LinkedIn. Again, nothing is accomplished. Way to many business people think they have actually done something.

This is why, with many, their business in year 5 looks a lot like their year one... lack of skills where it counts.

This Part Two is devoted to changing that scenario. It demonstrates how to turn, perhaps, previous failed "business" events into gold mines of great value. The only catch is that it requires actual work. 5% of those reading this (and hopefully more) will take the process to heart and are eager to explode their business. 95% will not. Be one of the 5%. This is your challenge.

Lasting progress won't be seen quickly, although strong results will be seen in a surprisingly short period of time. But by embracing and implementing this follow up plan; you will be known, liked, and trusted... a key ingredient to attracting clients, friend and referral partners.

Your circle of influence will expand. Business will flow your way!

Note: To paraphrase legendary business coach, Jim Rohn, success is easy; the tasks are easy to do. Concurrently, they are also easy not to do. All one has to do is a few easy things every day. This book is comprised of only easy things.

The Fortune is in the Follow Up!

Without a follow up plan that is implemented effectively, you might as well not start the process. Participating in networking events with the expectation that just showing up and swapping business cards will lead to significant business, is naïve at best!

WHY FOLLOW UP IS NECESSARY!

The stats tell the story.

Sales Statistics

48% of sales people never follow up with a prospect
25% of sales people make a 1st or 2nd contact and stop
12% of sales people only make 3 contacts and stop
- **Only 15% of sales people make more than 3 contacts**

- -

2% of sales are made on the 1st contact
3% of sales are made on the 2nd contact
5% of sales are made on the 3rd contact
10% of sales are made on the 4th contact
- **80% of sales are made on the 5th to 12th contact**

What a huge gap and opportunity! If you quit

after 2-3 follow up contacts, you miss out on the chance of doing business with 90% of the people you've met.

Make these stats work for you... there are no shortcuts. However, consistent perseverance pays off over time.

MAKE NOTE OF 2 BIG QUESTIONS!!!...

WHEN YOU...	DO YOU CALL...	ANSWER
Feeling sick	doctor you don't know?	Not a chance!
Toothache	dentist you don't know?	Not a chance!
Back hurts	chiro. you don't know?	Not a chance!
Need insurance	agent you don't know?	Not a chance!
Car needs repair	mechanic... don't know?	Not a chance!
Need a home loan	mortgage lender... ?	Not a chance!
Need a business loan	banker you don't know?	Not a chance!

YOU SELL _____, IF SOMEONE NEEDS IT, BUT DOESN'T KNOW AND RESPECT YOU, WOULD YOU GET THE SALE?

"NOT A CHANCE!"

Now is the time to be known, favorably... Now is the time to work on your networking skills / activity, and especially the activity that only 5% use... **EFFECTIVE FOLLOW UP!**

For your top Super Stars, now and in the future, the (20%) who account for 80% of your business... any success system must include a...

<u>ONE ON ONE</u>
(Your single most valuable tool for growth)

A fact of business is that we tend to do business with those that <u>we know</u>, those that <u>we like</u> and those that <u>we trust</u>. (A philosophy codified and championed for decadesby Ivan Miser, founder of Business Networking International).

The 'One on One' bridges the gap between being familiar with a partner/prospect, and truly being knowledgeable about what a partner does... and who he or she really is.

A 'One on One' is an offsite meeting (over coffee or over lunch during the normal business week) where you can exchange business and personal information with the objective of getting to really know the each other on a deeper level. Its purpose is for you to learn what constitutes a <u>good referral for them</u> and to get to know them well enough so that they come to mind immediately should someone you are talking with thereafter need their services.

It is suggested that you always ask what their goals are. This will uncover areas in which you can be helpful.

But, <u>never ask for referrals</u>! Each One on One is an opportunity to have a "referral conversation" however. (i.e. your goal might be to give 2 referrals and receive 1 referral each week, or give 50 referrals and receive 25 referrals this year) This makes the subject mutual; not self-serving

What a 'One on One' is not. A <u>'One on One' is not a time to try to sell something</u>. It is considered rude and selfish to do so, not to mention unproductive, to launch into a sales pitch. Following a sales pitch approach only alienates the other person. Trying to make a sale is just silly, not to mention self defeating. And you are cut off from ever doing business with their contacts.

If a person has a sphere of influence of 100-200 people that group knows 100-200 people ech, those initial contacts represent access to up to 40,000 people. Providing service and gaining access to that broad group is a long term purpose of the 'One on One' networking activity. Therefore, treating each other as a counselor and guide is much more productive. If they know, like and trust you… you will have entry into the lives of those they know.

As a guide, if you have questioned and listened 80% of the time, and have gotten to know more about the other person ("F.O.R.M."), and know what would be a good referral for them, then you have had a very successful 'One on One.' You have an open door to future conversations. If you've talked 80% of the time, you're probably toast. Dominate the listening!

NOTE: I make it a personal goal to leave each One on One with at least one personal assignment in which I can be of service to him/her for which I am committed to complete within the next 7 days.

Important Warning

Both Part 1 and Part 2 of this book suggest actions to be taken; tasks to accomplish. They are important. However, they are actions not merely to be marked off a check list and considered done.

They must have meaning to the other person. You are striving to make real human contacts, to build lasting relationships... to be of value, of service. Don't just be friendly, be a friend.

Be coming from the heart. Make real emotional connections. To do that one needs to be humble, empathetic, open, vulnerable and appreciative. i.e.

- If you are dropping off a business article relative to their industry, share why it is meaningful to you.
- If you are inviting them to coffee, share a story as to how it was of mutual interest to someone in the past.
- If you are calling just to acknowledge a contact, include the value of the connection to you that is edifying.

Make each contact special, not perfunctory. Express a genuine interest because there is a genuine interest.

In other words, the suggestions contained herein are not formulas of activity. They are methods and suggestions for making contacts and for making each contact special.

Important: Let's Look at a Study in Contrasts

'TONY' and 'ALICE'

Two sales people in town with completely Different stories worth studying!

TONY and ALICE BOTH...

Live in the same town, sell the same product, work for the same company, joined the company at the same time, went to the same school, have the same training, same this, same that, etc., etc... except:

Tony has a Problem.

- His business is not growing.
- Clients leave as fast as Tony adds new ones.
- Tony is perceived as interested only in the sale.
- He is eager but self absorbed.

Alice on the Other Hand.

- Has a booming business.
- Seems to be friends with everyone.
- Is known for her appreciation and edification of clients and prospects.
- Grows her business mostly through referrals.

The Difference... We can learn from what they do.

The Alice Philosophy

Alice believes each of us is unique, special and worthy of praise and edification. She also knows it is important to take the time to express this appreciation consistently in a physical way so others can see, touch and feel that appreciation!

This Appreciation Evokes the Law of Attraction:

- Do all the good you can, in all the ways you can, in all the places you can, at all the times you can, to all the people you can, for as long as you can. (John Wesley)

- In her business, Alice's follow up plan does just that... consistently lets people know they are appreciated and important.

Alice has a plan. She knows that 80% of her business comes from, or will come from, a small percentage of her clients and prospects. She focuses on those high value clients and prospects.

Her "Red Velvet" rope policy is to only associate with positive people of personal talent and integrity for whom she can maximize her value.

Tony (you may recognize Tony)... His Follow Up is:

- Swapping business cards... and that's about it.
- Sending a "Nice to Meet You" email, maybe
- Adds name to his group email lists, maybe
- Makes one phone call, maybe
- Goes to the next networking event equally and totally unprepared.

Contrast with Alice... Her Follow Up

- Same as Tony (except she does it), PLUS...
- Stops by the office the next day
- Sends a "Nice to Meet You" real greeting card
- Phones monthly to "just check in"
- Initiates "One on One" Coffee meetings regularly.

- ... PLUS
- Sends birthday, holiday and 'just because' cards
- Initiates a 'Netweaving'(1) luncheon with another synergistic person of value (becomes a connector)
- Drops off gifts or information of value
- Gives referrals often
- Takes prospect/client to lunch annually

(1)See page 170. The Little Black Book of Connections by Jeffery Gitomer for "Netweaving."

Who Would You Do Business With or Refer Business to: Tony or Alice?

Which One Are You More Likely To KNOW - LIKE - TRUST?

FOLLOW UP PYRAMID OF SUCCESS
(It's not crowded at the Top)

Your Activity Pyramid to Create
Committed Clients and Strategic Referral Partner Super
Stars, includes Seven Specific Levels.

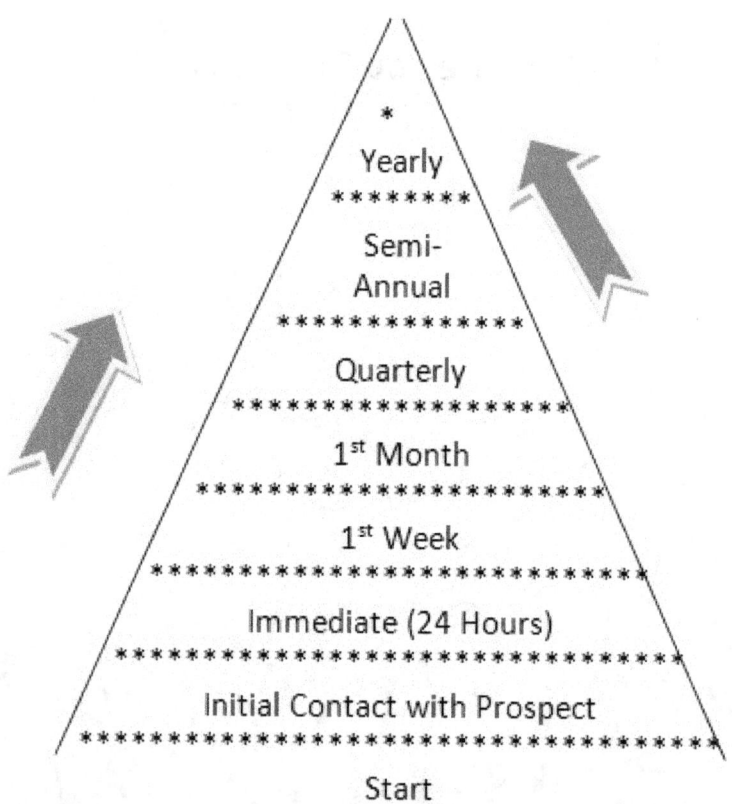

*
Yearly
* * * * * * * *
Semi-
Annual
* * * * * * * * * * * *
Quarterly
* * * * * * * * * * * * * * * *
1st Month
* * * * * * * * * * * * * * * * * * *
1st Week
* *
Immediate (24 Hours)
* *
Initial Contact with Prospect
* *
Start
Taking Strangers to Committed Clients & Partners

Annual Cost of Effective Follow Up:

Email, social media, phone calls	zero
7 Greeting cards a year	$ 10.00
Gifts, books, something of value	$ 20.00
Annual lunches	$ 40.00
Total	$ 70.00

Would you invest your time and $70.00 per year on each of your top 10 prospects and clients? <u>Someone will</u>!

It is a lot less expensive to keep a client than it is to generate a new one, plus you are building, not playing catch up.

The Real Message Here is:
Alice "Earns Referral Business" Daily!
She Doesn't Ask. It Naturally Flows Her Way.

And Tony with his current 'non' system doesn't stand a chance. He'll just keep showing up to event after event wondering why his life is so hard! While there he most likely will also do something that alienates every one!

<u>Follow Up is a Daily Skill</u>,

not just a social activity.

<u>Alice gets it and does the work</u>!

Tony Doesn't!

Time to get real and look in the mirror with the delusion glasses off. What is <u>Your Plan</u> for a new prospect? Are you serious about building your business?

Actions provide the answer! Plans for...

- 1st 24 hours?
- 1st week?
- 1st month and thereafter?
- 1st quarter and thereafter?
- 1st 6 months?
- Annually?
- 1st 5 years?

<u>CRITICAL</u>: Always schedule time daily on your calendar for follow up. No calendar time = no follow up.

Also, as we said before, if you schedule attending an event, concurrently schedule/calendar follow up time. If not, stay home and save your time and money.

YOUR WORKBOOK PLAN

Alice's plan for First 24 Hours...

1. Sends complimentary email (1)
2. Sends personalized gratitude card, real, not digital
3. Friend on Facebook, Google+ and LinkedIn
4. Adds to email (1) & Constant Contact lists
5. Visits their web site and leaves positive comments
6. Sends a brief text.

Your 1st 24 Hour Follow Up Plan:

_____

_____

_____

_____

_____

(1) Note, an email has almost zero value. 72% are never opened and those that are, are rarely read. They do virtually nothing to build relationships. Don't count email as one of your contacts.

Hello My Name Is Wayne

Wayne R. Weld   Page 50

**Alice's plan for First Week Follow up…
this is already past what 80% will do!**

1. Visits office
2. Schedules a One on One coffee meeting
3. Calls with information of interest to them
4. Sends a book or something of value

Your 1st Week Follow Up Plan:

_____

_____

_____

_____

_____

_____

_____

_____

_____

Alice's plan for Monthly Follow Up:

1. Sends information of value on their personal or business interests.
2. Sends normal newsletter, e-zine, etc.
3. Calls to 'just catch up.'
4. Send a Gratitude card.

Your 1st Monthly Follow Up Plan:

_____

_____

_____

_____

_____

_____

_____

_____

_____

Alice's plan for Quarterly Follow Up:

1. <u>Gives</u> prospects/clients a referral
2. Phones prospect to 'catch up'
3. Sends prospect a 'just because' greeting card (includes their picture).

Your 1st Quarterly Follow Up Plan:

_____

_____

_____

_____

_____

_____

_____

_____

_____

Alice's Plan for Semi Annual Follow Up:

1. Sends a real, in the mail, heartfelt card of appreciation
2. Gifts a book or something of value
3. Phones to 'catch up'
4. Takes as a guest to a business seminar event

Your Semi Annual Follow Up Plan:

_____

_____

_____

_____

_____

_____

_____

_____

_____

Alice's Plan for Annual Follow Up:

1. Takes prospect/client to lunch (at a favorite restaurant)
2. Sends birthday cards (to spouse and kids too), Holiday and 'just because' cards.
3. Takes client/partner to an industry or personal development seminar. (i.e. Tony Robbins)

Your Annual Follow Up Plan:

_____

_____

_____

_____

_____

_____

_____

Alice's Continuing Action Steps (for the next 2-5 years) **for exceptional prospects/clients**:

1. Periodic dissemination of valuable material.
2. Quarterly or semi-annual appreciation cards.
3. Sends Birthday and other unexpected greeting cards.
4. Quarterly phone calls just to check in.
5. Meets for coffee regularly.
6. Takes to lunch annually.
7. Gives Client/Prospect referrals regularly.
8. Buys a year's subscription to a favorite magazine.

Your Continuing Action Follow Up Plan:

_____

_____

_____

_____

_____

_____

No, you don't have to do everything that Alice does...
But you do have to have a complete, rigorous,
comprehensive plan that is created by you, tailored for
you, and is personally implemented by you.

YOUR TOP 8 PERSONAL FAVORITE AND MOST EFFECTIVE FOLLOW UP ACTIVITIES:

1 _____

2 _____

3 _____

4 _____

5 _____

6 _____

7 _____

8 _____

Review - Possible Follow Up Ideas

(give special attention to your few "A" List Super Stars)

- Add to email list, add to Constant Contact
- "Friend" on Facebook / LinkedIn
- Send periodic real Greeting Cards (birthdays / special occasions)
- Visit their web site and make favorable comments; review semi annually for possible testimonials
- Write a review on Facebook & LinkedIn
- Send brief texts
- Visit their office 1-2 times a year
- Schedule a One-on-One within the 1st week then semi-annually
- Call from time to time to "check in" and provide information of value
- Stop by office with a gift book
- Send normal newsletter, e-zine, etc.
- Give referrals as often as possible
- Take as guest to a business seminar
- Send an unexpected card of gratitude from time to time
- Gift a magazine subscription of activities of personal interest
- Gift 2 tickets to a cultural or entertainment event
- Take to lunch periodically
- Give referrals as often as possible (this is a duplicate on purpose)
- Attend charity events or meetings they sponsor
- Schedule a "Netweaving" encounter with other possible referral partners
- Acknowledge any special honors or accomplishments
- Your ideas; what would you appreciate?

Planned Out-Come
of Being Selective Over Time.

This is the math on effective follow up... building to 50 clients/referral partners you can expect to be generating significant business with; probably over 80% of your income.

Referral Activity Math		
If you attend	2	Meeting / Mo.
and meet	2	Super Star Possibilities / Meeting
You will follow up with	4	Super Star Possibilities / Month
which gives you	48	New Super Star Possibilities / Year
success rate at 20%	9.6	Success Rate Round up to 10
and		You Continue for 5 Years
Your group of Super Stars will be	48	Total # of Super Stars Referring You Business.

These 48-50 partners will help you create a sustainable booming business.

Question: Would you rather casually know 100 people, or get regular referrals from 5-10?

The answer is obvious.

Don't be a Chamber of Commerce junkie or Networking Groupie... where you just show up looking for business... handing out your card and telling people what you do. The stink of that will follow you for a long time.   Show up with the idea of being of service.

You don't need to go to dozens and dozens of events and meet hundreds of people.

 Instead, show up intentionally with a plan looking for ways to provide exceptional value in helping others grow their business.

Participate in 1-2 events a month and make 1-2 meaningful contacts per event. Have a follow-up plan for immediately following up; then continuously following up over time. Just do this and you will grow your real sphere of influence significantly.

With this system, imagine what your business would be like in 5 years!

Rule #1: <u>**The Fortune is in the Follow Up**</u>.

Rule #2: <u>**There is No Rule #2**</u>! **See Rule #1.**

To paraphrase Jeffery Gitomer from his "Little Black Book of Connections" it's not how many people you know, it's how many connected people know you, favorably."

Be one of the five (5%)
Out of 100 that gets it right!

<u>Your Fortune Awaits</u>!

Appendix

Suggested Reading Recommendations.

Study of Written Communication Success Rates.

A Simple Tool You Can Use Effectively.

Suggested Information Gathering Forms.

> **F.O.R.M.**
>
> **Follow Up Log**
>
> **Profile Questionnaire**

Author Biography.

<u>NOTE</u>: Many of the illustrations and forms used in this book are available to download, at no cost, on my website: **www.hellomynameiswayne.com**

Suggested Reading Recommendations:

Start Here...

"The Little Black Book of Connections" by Jeffery Gitomer
"The 7 Levels of Communication" by Michael J. Maher
"Straight-Line Leadership" by Dusan Dyukich

Continue...

"The Referral of a Lifetime" by Ken Blanchard
"Book Yourself Solid" by Michael Port
"How to Win Friends and Influence People" by Dale Carnegie
"The Slight Edge" by Jeff Olson
"Personality Plus" by Florence Littauer
"The Fred Factor" by Mark Sanborn
"The Go-Giver" by Bob Burg
"Excuse Me, Your Life is Waiting" by Lynn Grabhorn
"The E Myth Revisited' by Michael Gerber
"Eat That Frog" by Brian Tracy
"The Magic of Thinking Big" by David Schwartz
"Start with Why" by Simon Sinek
"What Great Salespeople Do" By Michael Bosworth & Ben Zoldan

"Insight Selling" by Michael Harris
"Wild at Heart" by John Eldredge
"The Master Key System" by Charles T. Haanel

I highly recommend these books to gain skills and insights into business success, sales success and growth in personal development.

Reading is the path to knowledge.   If experience is the best teacher, why not learn from others. In 2-3 hours you can learn a lifetime of someone else's experience. In a single year you can benefit from the lessons learned through experience taught by dozens of successful women and men.

Conversely, as observed by Jim Rohn, "those who do not read are no better off than those who cannot read."

A quick analysis of written communication effectiveness.

Communication Effectiveness - 2013

Communication Vehicle	Open Rate	Click-Thru Rate	Saved for 1+ Week	
Regular Email	28.5%	4.3%	0.0%	*
Email Newsletter	15.0%	2.6%	0.0%	*
Blog Post	12.0%	NA	0.0%	*
Text Message	98.0%	NA	0.0%	*
Real Greeting Card	98.0%	98.0%	85.0%	**

*   Source: MarketingProfs 1/17/14

** Personal Observation

A Simple Tool You Can Use Effectively

We all look for efficient/ effective ways to keep in touch with people. There are many tools, as we have discussed, to assist in follow up; i.e. the internet, social media, One-on-Ones, real greeting cards, lunches, office visits, phone calls, seminar attendance, newsletters, etc.

For me, one particular tool stands out for businesses; the greeting card and gifting possibilities provided by **Send Out Cards**. It is the number one business follow up system and relationship marketing system in the world. You can begin using it immediately.

Consider the following credentials of the eleven year young company:

- Largest user of 1st class stamps in the country from the US Postal Service.
- As of 1/1/2015 over 120,000,000 cards sent.
- As of 1/1/2015 over 5,000,000 gifts sent.
- Over 70% of the above sent by businesses.
- #1 company in the world in pre-scheduled multi-touch campaigns.
- The world leader in Relationship Marketing.

If you are using real greeting cards (thank you's, birthdays, anniversaries, gratitude, etc), or plan to, and are not using the **Send Out Card** services the following should be of interest:

- Through an on line business account, a real through the

- Mail, personal greeting card can be sent in about a minute.
- All customizable, including pictures and gifts.
- Cost is just over $1.00 a card (plus postage).
- Personal follow up single or multi-card campaigns can be created in minutes that go to 10's, 100's or 1,000's with a single key stroke. Can include gifts.
- The contact manager reminds you in advance of birthdays, anniversaries and other dates you ask for.
- It is a physical representation of appreciation that is treasured by the recipient; impact of receiving a personal card with a couple of brownies is stunning.

Should you be curious as to what the buzz is about and how to more easily establish your market presence using relationship marketing, be my guest in sampling the **Send Out Cards** system.

Send one free card today on me to someone you care about and observe the effect..

Simply access**: new.SendOutCards.com/LTD** and follow the instructions to "Send A Card," or call me and I will walk you through it.

Discover for yourself what a powerful tool **Send Out Cards** is, and how unbelievably cost effective it is as well.

I can tell you from personal experience that a person who receives a card with their picture keeps it for a long long time!

F.O.R.M. (Family, Occupation, Recreation, Motivation or Money)
Conversational Topics – First Contacts

Initial conversations with prospective clients/referral partners can follow a format that creates a personal history quickly. You can learn a lot in 3-5 minutes. Be ready to answer the same questions yourself.

Remember the term **F.O.R.M.** (1) as an easy way to remember the questions and sequence.

1. <u>Family and Friends:</u>

Are you married?
Do you have children?
Do you have brothers and sisters?
Where did you grow up?
How did you end up here?
Do you like it here?

2.   <u>Occupation:</u>

What kind of work do you do? How long have you been doing that?

What do you like most about your job?
How did you get into this career?
What is the most challenging part of your job?
Is this your dream job? If not, what might be?

3. Recreation:

When you have time, what do you like to do for fun?
How do you unwind after a long day?
What's your favorite sport or pastime?
What kind of music do you like?
Where do you or would you like to vacation? Why there?
Do you have a favorite restaurant in town?

The sequence of categories is important as answering motivation and money questions may be more difficult and you will want to make sure that you have already covered significant ground. However, should you get motivation or money answers you will also find out the most about what makes them feel satisfied and what gives their life meaning.

4. Motivation or Money:

Aside from work and leisure, what are you passionate about?

How did you develop a passion for that?
If you didn't have to work, what would you do?

F.O.R.M will help you get off to a good start in building a relationship. With the Super Stars you uncover, be sure to implement a full follow up plan.

(1)   Thanks to www.NetworkMarketingDreamTeam.com for parts of this forma

Relationship Marketing That Works!

* * FOLLOW UP LOG - 1ST YEAR * * *

HELLO
Wayne

Name: _____ Date _____

First 24 Hours	Actions	Dates
First Week	Actions	Dates
First Month	Actions	Dates
First Quarter	Actions	Dates
1st 6 Months	Actions	Dates
2nd 6 Months	Actions	Dats
First Year	Actions	Dates

His/Her Areas of Interest	

(Sample)

CLIENT/PROSPECT PROFILE INFORMATION

(Get to know the real person on an authentic level.)

The objective is to continuously gather information on each prospect so that, over time, this profile becomes complete and it is clear as to how you can provide optimal service.

Date: _____

Last Update _____

By _____

Client/Prospect

Name _____ **Nickname** _____

Title _____

Company Name & Mailing Address

_____

_____

Email Address

_____

Telephone   Business_____

Home _____

Cell _____

Birth Date & Place _____

Hometown _____

Relationship Marketing That Works!

Height _____ Weight _____

Outstanding Physical Characteristics _____

What can I do to be the most helpful in this relationship?

_____

_____

_____

Education

High School & Year _____

College _____ Degrees _____

College Honors _____

Advanced Degrees _____

College Fraternity/Sorority _____

College Extracurricular Activities _____

If he/she did not attend college, what instead

_____

Military Service (Branch) _____

Discharge Rank _____

Attitude towards being in the Military _____

Family

Marital Status _____ Spouse Name _____

Spouse Education _____

Spouse Interests / Activities / Affiliations _____

_____

Wedding Anniversary _____

Children Names /Ages / Educations /Hobbies

_____ _____

_____

_____

_____

Business Background
Previous Employment / Career (Most Recent First)

Company

_____

Location_____

Dates _____ **Title** _____

Company

_____

Location_____

Dates _____ **Title** _____

Company

_____

Location_____

Dates _____ **Title** _____

Status Symbols in Office _____

Professional or Trade Associations _____

Office or Honors in Them _____

Attitude Towards His/her Company _____

Relationship Marketing That Works!

Long Range Business Objective _____

Immediate Business Objective _____
What is of the Greatest Concern to the Prospect at the Moment

_____

Top 3 PERSONAL Goals Short Term

_____

_____

_____

Top 3 PERSONAL Goals Long Term

_____

_____

_____

Special Interests

Clubs or Service Clubs (Masons, Kiwanis, etc.) _____

_____

Confidential Items NOT to be discussed (Divorce, AA, etc.)

_____

What subjects (outside of business) are there strong feelings?

_____

Medical History (current condition of health) _____

_____

_____ ____

Drink? _____   How Much? _____
Favorite Place for Lunch _____
Favorite Place for Dinner _____

Hello My Name Is Wayne

Favorite Menu Item? _____

Hobbies & Recreational Interests _____

_____

Favorite Books and Reading Subjects _____

_____

Vacation Habits _____

Spectator Sport Interests (sports / teams) _____

_____

Kind of car (s) _____

Conversational Interests _____

Who is he/she Anxious to Impress _____

What Adjectives Best Describe him/her? _____

Personality Type (color) _____

Proudest Achievements _____

_____

Prospect/Client and Me

Moral or Ethical Considerations Involved with Working with
Him/Her _____

Concerned About the Opinion of Others _____

Self Centered _____ Highly Ethical _____

What are the Key Problems as he/she sees them: _____

_____

_____

_____

_____

What Can I Do to be the Most Helpful in the Relationship?

_____

_____

_____

_____

(Source: The MACAY 66)

Relationship Marketing That Works!

Author Biography - Wayne Weld

Wayne Weld, with successful careers in Real Estate, Insurance, Franchising, Commodities and Financial Planning to his credit, lives in Tucson, AZ. He is a long time advocate of building lasting business relationships and strategic alliances through relationship marketing.

Mr. Weld is a graduate of Ohio University with a degree in Economics and English and treasures his time doing undergraduate work at Dartmouth College and post graduate work at Stanford University Graduate Business School.

Wayne currently leads a premier business networking group in Tucson, "Networking Entrepreneurs of Tucson," and started other successful networking groups, including BNI (Business Networking International) chapters in Orange County CA and Tucson.

Mr. Weld sees a universal lack of consistent effectiveness in business networking. He attributes this lack of results to, 1) deficient networking skills, and 2) inadequate follow-up skills. This book is created so you can learn and embrace a professional skills approach to networking and relationship marketing, thereby achieving awesome results.

Wayne is an Air Force veteran who today loves to walk, hike, golf, read, and meet people One-on-One over coffee. Wayne runs his own greeting card and gifting business, www.sendoutcrds.com/LTD. Its primary purpose is bringing people closer together. As you will see, appreciation and edification are key to facilitating meaningful lasting relationships.

.

new.sendoutcards.com/LTD * 520-240-4552 * wweld@comcast.net